This journal is a gift to:

____

From:

____

Date:

____

My Life, My Story

A MOTHER'S
LEGACY JOURNAL

Christian art gifts®

Visit Christian Art Gifts website at www.christianartgifts.com.

My Life, My Story
A Mother's Legacy Journal

Published by Christian Art Gifts, Inc.

First edition 2019

Editorial development by Todd Hafer

Designed by Allison Sowers

Cover and interior images used under license from Shutterstock.com.

ISBN 978-1-64272-638-1

Printed in China

28 27 26 25 24 23

10 9 8 7 6 5 4 3 2 1

Contents

Introduction

Every mother has a story. It is time for me to share mine.

In my life, I have learned so many things about what is truly important, including the love, laughter, and legacies that families share and pass on from generation to generation.

As life moves along, memories become one's constant companions, but they can also be gifts—gifts meant to be shared with those you love. Gifts that celebrate the enduring bonds of family.

As I share my life with you in these pages, I will pass on the wisdom, values, and memories that have graced my days—with the hope that, somehow, reading my story will help you write yours, beautifully and meaningfully.

With love,

Me: at a glance

"Before you were conceived, I wanted you.
Before you were born, I loved you.
Before you were here an hour,
I would die for you.
This is the miracle of life."

Maureen Hawkins

Here is the story of the where and when of my birth . . .

My full given name is . . .

My name was chosen by . . .

I was given this name because . . .

The first nickname I can remember was . . .

I earned this nickname because . . .

My mom's full name and place of birth are . . .

My dad's full name and place of birth are . . .

As for siblings and their birthplaces . . .

My maternal grandparents are . . .

My paternal grandparents are . . .

My husband's full name and place of birth are . . .

As for my children and their birthplaces . . .

I will wait for the LORD . . .
I will put my hope in Him.
I and the children
the LORD has given me . . .

Isaiah 8:17-18

A few of my favorite things

"True, a mother has many cares.
But they are sweet cares."

Juliette Montague Cook

My favorite way to spend a day is . . .

As a child, my favorite TV show was . . .

But now, my favorite is . . .

If there is one movie I can watch over and over, it's . . .

I love this movie because . . .

My favorite sport is . . .

I like this sport best because . . .

My favorite team is . . .

My favorite athlete is . . .

My all-time favorite vacation place is . . .

I love vacationing here because . . .

If I could eat only one food for the rest of my life, it would be . . .

My "guilty pleasure" when it comes to food is . . .

My all-time favorite song is . . .

Here's what makes this song special to me:

My favorite activity is . . .

This activity is tops because . . .

A perfect night out for me would have to include . . .

The skill I'm most proud of is . . .

I first knew I had this ability when . . .

People tell me my best trait is . . .

In my opinion, my best trait is . . .

If I could change anything about myself, it would probably be . . .

A typical day for me is sure to include . . .

"Your heavenly Father already knows all your needs.
Seek the Kingdom of God above all else,
and live righteously & He will give you everything
you need. So don't worry about tomorrow."

Matthew 6:32-34

My life as a little girl

"There is a garden in every childhood,
an enchanted place where colors are
brighter, the air is softer, and the morning
more fragrant than ever again."

Elizabeth Lawrence

Here's what I remember most about my childhood home . . .

When I recall my bedroom, here's the picture that comes to mind . . .

If you could walk through my old neighborhood, here's what you'd see:

That neighborhood is different today because . . .

My childhood best friend was . . .

We got along because . . .

As a child, my favorite thing to do was . . .

My *least* favorite thing, on the other hand, was . . .

If I was a child prodigy at anything, it was . . .

My fondest wish as a kid was . . .

My favorite childhood toy was . . .

My favorite book was . . .

Back then, my favorite place to be was . . .

I loved that place because . . .

If you were looking for me and my friends, you'd most likely find us . . .

As for my religious foundation and childhood memories of church . . .

The scent that always takes me back to my childhood is . . .

My most treasured childhood memory is . . .

The childhood experience that influenced me most was the time . . .

You made all the delicate,
inner parts of my body and knit me
together in my mother's womb.
Thank You for making me
so wonderfully complex!
Your workmanship is marvelous—
how well I know it.

Psalm 139:13-14

My family life

"Every child born into the world
is a new thought of God,
an ever-fresh and radiant possibility."

Kate Douglas Wiggin

When my mom was younger, she looked like . . .

If you entered our house, you'd most likely find my mom . . .

When my dad was younger, he looked like . . .

If my dad had a catchphrase back in those days, it would probably be . . .

As best as I can remember, my mom spent her days . . .

My favorite thing to do with my dad was . . .

I'm like my dad because . . .

But, Dad and I are different when it comes to . . .

It's hard to believe that my dad used to . . .

If my mom had a catchphrase back in those days, it would probably be . . .

When I was a child, my dad's occupation was . . .

My opinion of Dad's job was . . .

As a child, my favorite family activity was . . .

My favorite childhood memory of my mom is . . .

I'm like my mom because . . .

I'm different from my mom because . . .

The best way to describe our economic status back then would be . . .

As for household responsibilities, my parents insisted that I always . . .

My parents encouraged me by . . .

A couple of my all-time favorite family memories are . . .

When it came to getting along with my family members, I was . . .

As for childhood pets, my favorite was . . .

Here's what I miss most about being a child . . .

My earliest memories of my grandparents are . . .

My favorite memories of visiting my grandparents, or their visits to me, are . . .

Here's what I loved most about my grandparents . . .

One valuable lesson I learned from my grandfather or grandmother is . . .

What I know or remember about my great-grandparents is . . .

Some things I know about my family history and my ancestors are . . .

The aunts, uncles, and/or cousins I have been closest to are . . .

At family reunions, I . . .

The strangest relative I've ever met was . . .

My favorite home-cooked meal was . . .

The snacks and special treats I remember my family enjoying together were . . .

When my family had company, I . . .

My favorite place to eat when my family dined out was . . .

Here's why I loved that place . . .

When I was a child, weekends were . . .

On family summer outings, we usually . . .

During the winter, my family and I liked to . . .

When I think of my family, the first words that come to mind are . . .

Direct your children onto the right path, and when they are older, they will not leave it.

Proverbs 22:6

My education

"Knowledge is the power that
gives us wings to soar."

Anonymous

I attended elementary school at . . .

My earliest memory of school is . . .

In elementary school, the things I enjoyed most were . . .

The things I enjoyed *least* were . . .

I attended middle school at . . .

I attended high school at . . .

My all-time favorite school subject was . . .

My favorite extracurricular activities were . . .

A memorable award I received in school was . . .

My memories of my favorite teacher are . . .

Some of the fashion trends during my school days were . . .

In my yearbook's senior-class photo, I look like . . .

Some popular songs I remember are . . .

Some movies I remember seeing include . . .

Some television shows I enjoyed are . . .

When I was a teenager, the big celebrities were . . .

Some things I remember about learning to drive are . . .

My first car was . . .

At dances and/or parties, I usually . . .

The biggest challenge of my teen years was . . .

If I had to relive my high school years, this time I would . . .

During high school, my goals and aspirations were . . .

After graduating from high school, I decided to . . .

I am so glad I did not decide to . . .

When I moved away from home, I . . .

My first dorm room or apartment was . . .

My favorite memories of college are . . .

Today, my connection to college is . . .

Those who search will surely find me.

Proverbs 8:17

Me: on the job

"A mother could perform the jobs
of several air-traffic controllers with ease."

Lisa Alther

When I was growing up, I wanted to be . . .

My first job was . . .

My first career-oriented job was . . .

When I first got this job, I felt . . .

The things I liked about this job were . . .

The most enjoyable job I ever had was . . .

The worst job I ever had was . . .

The most memorable place my work has taken me is . . .

A co-worker or boss who was a valuable mentor to me was . . .

An experience I had in mentoring someone else was . . .

Some valuable friendships I gained through my work were . . .

The most important things I've learned about life through my career . . .

Work willingly at whatever you do,
as though you were working
for the Lord rather than for people.

Colossians 3:23

My love story

"Alone we can do so little;
together we can do so much."

Helen Keller

My first crush was . . .

I attended my first boy/girl party when . . .

Here's what I recall about my first kiss . . .

Here's what I remember most about my first date . . .

A typical teen date usually included . . .

My first true love was . . .

I met my spouse when . . .

My first impression of him was . . .

The qualities I admired most in my future husband were . . .

As we got to know each other better, I learned . . .

The length of our courtship was . . .

Our favorite date-night activity was . . .

I knew I had found "the one" when. . . .

Here's what was most memorable about the marriage proposal:

Our wedding took place . . .

I wore . . .

My spouse wore . . .

A few of the most-special guests included . . .

Our "first dance" song was . . .

My fondest memory of my wedding day is . . .

For the honeymoon, we went to . . .

Right after getting married, we lived . . .

A typical evening during my early years of marriage was usually . . .

I first began thinking about having children when . . .

My closest friends from those early marriage years were . . .

The leisure activities I came to enjoy in married life were . . .

To me, here is what is most rewarding about marriage:

To maintain a healthy marriage, I think it is important to . . .

A time in my marriage when I learned the true value of teamwork was . . .

Today, here's what I value most about married life:

Two people are better off than one,
for they can help each other succeed.

Ecclesiastes 4:9

My life as a parent

"We find delight in the beauty
and happiness of children that makes
the heart too big for the body."

Ralph Waldo Emerson

When I first learned I was going to become a parent, I . . .

On the day my first child was born, I felt . . .

The significance behind my children's names is . . .

Having a newborn at home changes your daily life because . . .

Becoming a parent changed my outlook on life by . . .

My fondest memory from my early years of motherhood is . . .

The most fun a mom and dad can have with a young kid or two is . . .

When my spouse and I needed child-free entertainment, we . . .

My children are similar to me because . . .

My children are different because . . .

The most important values a mom can pass on to her child are . . .

My greatest joy in being a parent has been . . .

My greatest challenge has been . . .

My children's upbringing was similar to mine because . . .

It was different from mine because . . .

Something I know now that I wish I had known in early parenthood is . . .

The thing I truly hope my children have learned from me is . . .

The most important thing I have learned from my children is . . .

Seek His will in all you do, and
He will show you which path to take.

Proverbs 3:6

A life worth celebrating

"If you want a happy family,
if you want a holy family,
give your hearts to love."

Mother Teresa

When I was young, my birthdays were usually . . .

My favorite birthday memory would have to be . . .

My all-time favorite birthday present was . . .

A special meal or dessert I liked to have on my birthday was . . .

The first holiday gathering I hosted was . . .

If I were to grade myself on this event, I'd receive a(n) . . .

My all-time favorite Christmas carol is . . .

Christmas is special to me because . . .

When I was a child, Christmas was usually . . .

A childhood Christmas memory that really stands out for me is . . .

A childhood Christmas tradition I have passed on to my family is . . .

The most meaningful Christmas for me as a parent was . . .

Things I will always thank God for are:

When I was a child, my favorite holiday was . . .

A favorite summertime memory is . . .

As a child, Valentine's Day usually meant . . .

Sing a new song to the Lord,
for He has done wonderful deeds.
His right hand has won a mighty
victory; His holy arm has
shown His saving power!

Psalm 98:1

My Life:
THE MAIN EVENTS

"Life is not measured by the
number of breaths we take,
but by the moments that
take our breath away."

Unknown

The happiest time of my life has been . . .

The saddest has been . . .

The busiest time of my life has been . . .

The most relaxed and carefree has been . . .

One event that really shaped my life was . . .

A political event that made a strong impression on me was . . .

So far, my life's proudest accomplishment has been . . .

An accident, major surgery, or prolonged illness I had to endure was . . .

A really difficult time endured by someone close to me was . . .

When I think of a tragic time in my life, I remember when . . .

The toughest decision I've ever had to make was . . .

My most memorable travel experience has been . . .

The first time I traveled by airplane was . . .

The farthest I've ever traveled from home is . . .

The most memorable place I've ever visited is . . .

Placing my faith in God has been a major event in my life . . .

A cause to which I have dedicated myself is . . .

My favorite competitive activity is definitely . . .

The award or honor I am most proud of is . . .

The most important invention of my lifetime has been . . .

The first time I helped someone in need was . . .

The scientific discovery that has changed my life most has been . . .

Since my childhood, here is how society has changed most . . .

One thing I would never change about the way I live life is . . .

One thing I wish I had done differently is . . .

My hopes for the world in the next 10 years are . . .

My hopes for me and my family in the next 10 years are . . .

"Anything is possible if a person believes."

Mark 9:23

My sources of inspiration

"Hold tenderly that which you cherish . . ."

Bob Alberti

The people who have made the biggest impact on my life are . . .

As a young person, when I needed guidance, I usually went to . . .

My faith in God has shaped my life . . .

A Scripture passage that has been meaningful in my life is . . .

If I could keep one family photo, it would be . . .

My most treasured material possession is . . .

I still get a lump in my throat whenever . . .

I know that my life's ultimate calling is . . .

When I was young, my role models were . . .

One famous person I truly admire is . . .

A public speaker I enjoyed hearing (or would like to hear) is . . .

The author or book that has most inspired me is . . .

Other ways that I find inspirational moments in my day include . . .

Notes & memories

Don't copy the behavior and customs of this world,
but let God transform you into a new person
by changing the way you think.

Romans 12:2

We know that God causes everything to work together for the good of those who love God and are called according to His purpose for them.

Romans 8:28

You keep track of all my sorrows. You have collected all my tears in Your bottle. You have recorded each one in Your book.

Psalm 56:8

Don't worry about anything; instead, pray
about everything. Tell God what you need,
and thank Him for all He has done.

Philippians 4:6

Feed the hungry, and help those in trouble.
Then your light will shine out from the darkness,
and the darkness around you will be as bright as noon.

Isaiah 58:10

"God loves a person who gives cheerfully."

2 Corinthians 9:7

If you would like to share how
this journal has encouraged you
or someone close to you,
we would love to hear from you.
Send us an email at:
Publisher@christianartgifts.com